02-03-23

THE CHOSEN NAMES

BY TAHER ADEL

بسم الله الرحمن الرحيم

THE CHOSEN NAMES

Published by
Sun Behind The Cloud Publications Ltd
PO Box 15889, Birmingham, B16 6NZ
This first edition published in hardback in 2023
Copyright Taher Adel 2023©
The moral right of the author has been asserted
All rights reserved
A CIP catalogue record of this book is available
from the British Library
Cover art by Ruby Jaffery
ISBN (print): 978-1-908110-83-1
ISBN (ebook): 978-1-908110-84-8

Printed by Mega Printing in Turkey

www.sunbehindthecloud.com
info@sunbehindthecloud.com
Instagram: @sunbehindcloud
Facebook: @sunbehindthecloud

And He taught Adam the names, all of them. He laid them before the angels and said, "Tell me the names of these if you are truthful."

They said, "Glory be to Thee! We have no knowledge save what Thou hast taught us. Truly Thou art the Knower, the Wise.

He said, "Adam, tell them their names." And when he had told them their names He said, "Did I not say to you that I know the unseen of the heavens and the earth, and that I know what you disclose and what you used to conceal?

Surah al-Baqarah, verses 31-33

ACKNOWLEDGEMENTS

I would like to thank my parents for instilling the love of the Prophet ﷺ and his progeny into every breathing moment of my upbringing, allowing me to see life through their light in every waking moment. Without them, this book would not have been possible.

PREFACE

Many of us have grown up glorifying these names, loving these names and pledging allegiance to these names in one form or another. In fact, many of these names have become our names and our children's names. But who are these divine individuals and why are their names such powerful reminders?

The Chosen Names is a poetic exploration of sixteen unassailable personalities from the Household of Mohammed ﷺ, from the Prophet himself to the awaited Saviour. It is an etymological deep dive into the virtues and divine characteristics of a progeny that is like no other in human history.

Each name tells a story, a wound, a revelation and a prophecy that can be a book in itself but my job as a poet has been to distill their meaning and sentiment into beautiful verses of poetry that can act as reminders for us all. Most of these personalities have more titles and names than what it is included in this book of poetry and certainly there are other personalities from the extended household that could have been explored in a similar light but I have personally selected the sixteen that have helped inspire my poetic journey from a fledgling poet to one that has become obsessed with each letter of their names.

CONTENTS

Names of Mohammed	8
Names of Fatima	16
Names of Ali	24
Names of Hassan	30
Names of Hussain	37
Names of Abbas	43
Names of Zainab	50
Names of al-Sajjad	57
Names of al-Baqir	61
Names of al-Sadiq	64
Names of al-Kadhim	68
Names of al-Ridha	71
Names of al-Jawad	75
Names of al-Hadi	78
Names of al-Askari	81
Names of al-Mahdi	84

*I searched for meaning
and found that your life was poetry
I read your words and found the truth
placed between the letters of your names.*

NAMES OF MUHAMMAD

المصطفى

THE CHOSEN

Blessings upon the light chosen to radiate both
the heavens and the earth.
Blessings upon the name chosen to reverberate
through eternity in verse.

الحبيب

THE BELOVED

He is the celestial heart of the universe
Our creation is a love letter in motion
the moving parts of the orbit of devotion
like the earth itself praying on its axis
spinning with the planets
praising *His Beloved*.

THE TRUSTWORTHY

When they feared his revelation,
they could not question his character,
for he was like the *Quran*,
an open book.

SEAL OF PROPHETS

The inheritor, the seal, the origin,
the first and last nebula.
He walked as *Jesus* walked and talked as *Aaron* talked,
he fought as *David* fought and like *Moses* split seas
of discord with compassion and gentle thought.

COMPASSIONATE

The miracle born from a land where hearts
were as stubborn as the ground they walked on.
His birth was an oasis placed in the deserts
to save those drowning in droughts of hate and ignorance.

THE PERFECTLY COMPLETE

The words of God were arranged perfectly in his mind
and upon his tongue
but he was the unassailable burden of proof,
the living and breathing revelation
of the *Almighty*.

BEST OF MANKIND

We faced him like aching flowers
yearning for light
and when he passed, we deepened our roots
far and wide
searching for the remnants
of the best of mankind.

THE TRUTHFUL

The truth allotted itself entirely to settle under his care,
and like a father he would ensure
no truth was left unattended to
and no truth was orphaned in his presence.

الْرحمةُ لِلْعَالمين

THE MERCY TO MANKIND AND ALL CREATION

Just as we have sown the sun's light into each plant
we have sown his name into the delicate heart
of each child.
Just as the earth grows from beneath the sun's
fiery palms
his name will blossom its way to their lips in time.

THE CLOAKED ONE

He is God's cloaked secret on earth,
shrouded with *His* light
A secret spinning across the quilted fabric of time.

النُّور

THE LIGHT PERSONIFIED

When he arrived they said
the *full moon has appeared* because of the way
he walked the earth disarming darkness
with every step.

أَحْمَد

MOST DESERVING OF PRAISE

For the winds love to blow his name
from minarets to ears,
light enough to enter hearts
and weightless enough to find home
in our solemn tears.

PRASEWORTHY

His name is not made to burden you
nor tip your scales
it's made to lift you like oxygen
lifts atoms into air,
the essence of praise.

مُحَمَّد

PRAISED

And the final miracle was to carve his name
inside the beating heart of man.
A tongue may forget to sing his praises
but if the heart stops,
it dies.

NAMES OF FATIMA

THE PURE ONE

She, much like her father resembled purity on earth
a diamond ring placed around our equator
not measured in carats but chapters and verse.

ABUNDANCE

Her name is a heavenly river
and if it were to flow on earth
each never ending ripple would be a devotee
raised in her abundant care from birth.

الطاهرة

THE PURE AND CHASTE

Cloaked with the primordial light
she was the closest in purity
huddled as five, placed in thirty-three.

الزاهدة

THE DEVOUT

Lost in the worship of her Lord
a star swallowed
by the vastness
of the universe
She was at
the heart
of it
all.

سماوية

HEAVENLY

She walked between the cracks of the universe
yet she was not broken
twelve stars clung to her cloak, bees around a beacon
I looked between her hands and there embraced
the moon sat proud and swollen.

المحدثة

THE ONE WHOM THE ANGELS WOULD CONVERSE WITH

The angels would wait for her prayers
like forests would wait for rain.

سيدة نساء العالمين
CHOSEN LADY OF THE UNIVERSE

Words dissolve each time man mentions her name in wording
for no paper can find a pen to shoulder the burden.

العالية
THE ELEVATED

They could not find a celestial body to match her shining
except for the one man who would
equally tire pens from writing
For only *Ali* could match *Alia's* orbit.

الحبيبة

THE BELOVED

We swear upon her scent as roses pledge allegiance that no
fragrance touched the Prophet  but her presence.

ام ابيها

MOTHER OF HER FATHER

A nurturing shadow shielding the sun
shrouding it like a protective mother
or was it the eclipse of a loving daughter?

حانية

COMPASSIONATE

A heart soft, from base to core
starving herself to relieve the poor
Haniya, the open door
to sustenance, and even more.

THE TRUTHFUL

She was raised in the lap of *Al-Amin*
pressed firm against his loving heart
nurtured to the beat of infallibility
until each word she would say
became a prophetic
melody.

LADY OF LIGHT

She was paradise's native flora
Mohammed ﷺ in walk and aura
and when he was no more
she was a house of sorrow
a fading human aurora.

THE SEPARATOR

When the books close from left to right
I hope what is written is lost in her light.

NAMES OF ALI

ONE PLEASING TO GOD

A man who weighed
each action and intention
until his Lord was pleased.
A balancing act, whether striking his sword
or digging for divine mercy on knees.

FATHER OF DUST

He is the ground that we have burgeoned from
Children to the father of soil and dust
Seedlings growing at his heels
Infinitesimal motes trying to kneel.

BRAVE LION

His sword, a lion's claw
The valiant lifter of the door
Roaring from the moment his mother named him
to the moment his breaths left him.

ONE WHO ATTACKS REPEATEDLY

A hurricane of justice
placed between a two-pointed sword
no army can match this man
be it in battle or the whirling of words.

أَسَد ٱللّٰه

LION OF GOD

This lion and his sword
fears none but his Lord
until his mane would grey in worship
and his sword would blunt in searching.

أَمِير ٱلمُؤْمِنين

PRINCE OF BELIEVERS

The prince that every believer
will pledge his heart to
the crown jewel that we complete our faith to.

مظهر العجائب
MANIFESTATION OF WONDERS

The manifestation of wonders
Just like his birth, his name begets doors
that do not exist
splintering corners, defying physics.

أبو الأيتام
FATHER OF ORPHANS

A man who would soften his heart and
extend his nights
A man who would trawl the darkness
to father orphans.

لِسان آلله
TONGUE OF GOD

If words held earthly value,
his would produce diamond encrusted eloquence
His tongue shaped to slice through falsehood
dismantling evil and its skeletons.

علي
THE ELEVATED

A name that derives its meaning from height
for no soul can be elevated in station nor might
without recognising Ali for being *Ali*.

NAMES OF HASSAN

السبط

THE GRANDSON

One for each of the prophet's eyes,
two buds unfolding beneath *His* sky
the *grandson*, the spring after a long winter
and the tree is now as green as his dome.

السيد

THE DESCENDANT

When two lights act as a source
you form two young shadows
and he was poetry, his brother was prose
purifying the air like the Prophet's scented clothes.
He was musk and his brother was oud
for every person that saw them
was reminded of *Mahmood*.

سيد شباب أهل الجنة
LEADER OF THE YOUTH OF PARADISE

Dome or no dome,
paradise is his home
and the home of those who know.

التقي
THE GOD-CONSCIOUS

Each moment of his life was a promise
be it sword or paper, be it battle or treaty
in his hands they were both weapons of piety.

SHUBBAR

For even his name is a prophecy.
The sons of *Aaron* named
before *Moses* could split the sea,
before the pharaohs would ride their chariots,
before the mountains could even speak.

THE RIGHTEOUS

Placed in the palms of *His* beloved
with *Gabriel* in attendance,
how else did we expect him to grow?
A seed sown in fertile land
would always inherit *his* green.

THE ASCETIC

When in worship, you could not separate
this man from his Lord,
he was one with the earth's core
for he was the son of *Abu Turab*.

THE PRINCE

Not of wealth or throne
but of faith and hope,
of charity and growth.

الأمين
THE TRUSTWORTHY

Evil plotted and evil whispered
yet the more they did, the more they polished the mirror
until he was the perfect image of his Grandfather,
a source of trust even when the vultures hovered.

النقي
THE PURE

Like the purification of water
his love was now essential for survival.
The remnants of *Mohammed* , the expiators of sin
"No reward do I ask of you except the love of my kin."

المجتبى

THE CHOSEN ONE AMONG MANY

Like carefully selected flora
designed to withstand habitats
that seek to drain them of beauty
until their colours gleam through
even when pulled from root
and buried in unwelcoming domeless dirt.

HASSAN

The beauty of the flower is witnessed through
the petals that grow with her.
They are the concentration of *Zahra's* scent
and he was the first petal to drop.

NAMES OF HUSSAIN

السبط
THE GRANDSON

The roots that quench the leaves
and the leaves that nourish the roots
a symbiosis that cannot be split
for loving both is the stitching of the quilt
Hussain is a part of me and I am a part of him.

الراشد
THE RIGHTLY GUIDED

Be it the safety of *Medina* or the jaws of *Karbala*,
he surrendered his heart to *His Lord*
and so *His Lord* made it an everlasting shrine.
A compass for those who seek *Him*.

سيد شباب أهل الجنة
LEADER OF THE YOUTH OF PARADISE

He is the eternal smile found on the other side
the scent that lingers on like the touch of his shrine
He is youth after hardship and despair
after submission and sacrifice.

المبارك
THE BLESSED

He is the book of certainty written on the specks of time
usurping our hearts, seizing our souls
only to nourish and mesmerise.

الطيب
THE PURE

And even when the final remnant of the pure cloak
finds itself in distant lands torn piece by piece,
tattered and disfigured,
it will still be enough to cloak
generations to come, for purity cannot be uncovered.

الوفي
THE LOYAL

Even this name would shy away from his final moment.
With nothing more to give to *His Lord*,
he looked around for more, until nothing was left
but the purity of his own neck.

THE RIGHTEOUS

A heart caught between the crossfires of heaven and earth.
The earth was left to burn with the evil of the world
while heaven was uprooted to settle beneath his dust.

SHUBAYR

Like the two sons of *Aaron*,
the priesthood that upheld the virtues of *Moses*.
Saints whether they stand or sit.

ثار الله

BLOOD WHOSE AVENGER IS GOD

Each drop lost on that day would be accounted for
like precious pearls on the necklace on time,
they will be returned one by one to their Lord.

حسين

HUSSAIN

Revolution is the earnest student of his stand,
sacrifice is his fledgling apprentice,
while death is naive infant trailing behind
as he never dies.

NAMES OF ABBAS

قمر بني هاشم
HASHEMITE MOON

He did not need his father's double-edged sword to be great
for his double helix moved him
like the shadow of *Ali* in battle
and raised him like a moon in the cascades of darkness
until he was called the *Hashemite Moon*.

العميد
THE PILLAR

The making of *Abbas* was the mountain *Ali* sought after
Just like *Hajar* would run from Mount *Safa* to *Marwa*
to quench her child's thirst
Hussain sent his own mountain
from the river to his death.

حامل اللواء

THE FLAGBEARER

Zainab would look to the river and remember how the
desert wind caused the flag to shiver
No hand could calm the flag like the hand that calmed her
heart.

السقاء

THE WATER CARRIER

He waded in the water like the moon in eclipse
and whispered to his soul, forming tides with his lips
His hands were made to quench their thirst
but they ended up quenching the earth.

باب الحسين

DOOR OF HUSSAIN

On his brother's lap his head now rests
his tears like gems, lilies on broken stems
wilted, but not quite done,
a brother trying to drink his
last drop of sun.

باب الحوائج

DOOR OF WISHES

His hands were once forced empty by the riverbed,
now they open doors for our hopes and wishes.

حامي الظَّعينة
THE PROTECTOR

Where would their tears run to
without his shoulders to soak them
Where would their eyes flee to
without his shadow to shield them.

بطل العَلقمي
CHAMPION OF THE RIVER

He surrendered his arms in devotion
unfolding, open handed
His nobility saw him rest his soul by the river
because the ocean requested it.

العَابِد
THE WORSHIPPER

His forehead gleamed in worship
but now the sands dim this moon's resplendence.
A blood moon
carried on spears, a sacrifice to praying skies.

الشهيد
THE MARTYR

Said to be gifted with wings in the place
of the two hands he lost selflessly
trying to hold on to a promise until he had
no hands at all
and now here we come in droves
like river currents, looking for him.

الطيار

THE ONE THAT FLIES

The envy of angels, broad shoulders like pillars of temples
and wings in the place of hands that fell.
He could not fly to *Sukaina*
but his name will take flight in the heavens.

عباس

THE LION ALL OTHER LIONS FEAR

The Lion, the cub of the Lion
Abbas of the Hashemite pride
grew up as the plume of the House of *Ali*
yet he knelt before the sons of *Fatima*
draping his cape, lowering his feathers, sheathing his claws
a moon relinquishing his light
in total eclipse.

NAMES OF ZAINAB

عالمة غير المعلمة
UNTAUGHT SCHOLAR

She did not need to be taught,
for she was raised in the lap of eloquence.
Her home was the city of knowledge, but she did not need
to enter through its gate for she was the daughter of both its
King and Queen.

العقيلة
THE WISE

The pure would seek her counsel for she was the vestige of the cloak
human carnations hanging on every word
she spoke.

THE LEARNED

She was an encyclopaedia of patience
a teacher from behind the curtains of sadness
carrying pain and wisdom hostage
a library of loss and excellence.

THE TRUSTWORTHY

A beating heart positioned *Bayn Al-Haramayn*.
They lived for her, as she did for them.
The eternal flag pressed between her hands,
for even the future knew her by this name.

الحوراء
THE ONE WITH STRIKING BLACK EYES

This name is used to describe eyes that occupy
intense and beautiful darkness
eyes that have experienced tragedies but only
reflect beauty in light's absence.

نائبة الزهراء
REPRESENTATIVE OF AL-ZAHRA

Even her sadness reminded the people of *Zahra*.
Fatima had a house of sorrow built
but *Zainab* was a moving house
for her tears could not settle.

THE STRANGER

She became a stranger the moment she left them.
Her home is mourning with the masses,
she, just like her mother will find our *Majalis*,
the eternal resting place of the Queen of Damascus.

THE PURE

The cloak that purified her was stitched in layers
of pain until she too became
like her mother, a clean slate
crushed behind tyranny's door
too pure for life to burden anymore.

THE ELOQUENT

Honed by bravery and truth,
lionhearted eloquence reverberated
through the courts.
Her lips two pronged
like *Ali* in sword, she was in words.

HUSSAIN'S EQUAL

He was the prey of the swords
but she had to see it all
A living martyr who lived through each
wound but did not heal.

أُمّ المصائب
MOTHER OF CALAMITIES

Beneath the bleeding veils that separate the loved
eye from eye
beneath the quiet footprints in the sand
walking silent scars
beneath the chains that wrestle time
until they succumb to rust
beneath the skin that breaks and bones that shake
beneath the flesh that aches and heart that bakes
beneath it all
she saw nothing but beauty.

ZAINAB

When beauty was found unbowed
sacrificed without a shroud
when the truth was spoken aloud
and her presence silenced crowds
We saw nothing but *Zainab*.

NAMES OF AL-SAJJAD

زين العَابدين
ORNAMENT OF THE WORSHIPPERS

He is the best of worshippers, the best of tongues
He is eloquence found at its peak, the heart that speaks
in verse and divine soliloquy.
He is *Zainul Abideen*.

السجاد
THE PROSTRATOR

The son who unshackled himself
by chaining his head to the earth
lifting it only to unveil the skies
through words of soul piercing *dua*.

الامين
THE TRUSTWORTHY

Is there a man more worthy of trust
than the man who compiled the Treatise of Rights
and to adorn them all, he placed the seeker aloft.
The Right of Him Who Seeks Your Advice.

ابن الخيّرتين
SON OF THE BEST TWO

The son who reignited the fire of
Bani Hashem
after the vultures took their bite.
The son of Prophethood
and the viceregents by his side.

علي

ALI

The son who was the crowned Ali
after the first *Ali*
a reminder for the earth
to never forget his prostrating light.

NAMES OF AL-BAQIR

الباقر
THE ONE WHO SPLITS KNOWLEDGE

All seas are found where the ocean and land meet
so he must be an ocean when his mind opens and speaks
forming lakes and rivers mesmerising Rome and the Greeks,
a strike worthy of the son of eloquence's peak.

الهادي
THE GUIDE

He is the namesake of perfection
the grandson of his reflection
the fifth of fourteen
the answered prayer
of *Zainul Abideen*.

الشاكر

THE GRATEFUL

The remnants of *Bani Hashem* were left
with nothing to their names
but their gratitude to their Lord
raised them once again.

And we saw nothing but beauty

MOHAMMED

Revelation is found in his blood
and at the tip of his tongue.
Let it be known and let it be sung.

Praise be upon the son of the city
of knowledge and the son of its door.

NAMES OF AL-SADIQ

الصادق

THE TRUTHFUL

He spoke all the languages of the earth fluently
but none were as rich as the language of truth.
If truth be told, he was truth itself.

THE PATIENT

How does one defeat ignorance when it circles
you in the form of men?
How does one remain patient when the swords that
feasted on your ancestors now feast in words?
If the patience of *Zainab* defeated Yazid
then the patience of *Al-Sabir* guaranteed this victory.

الطاهر

THE PURE

He was a purity untaught,
chasteness unbought.
He was not just a teacher for all,
he was a living school of thought.

الفاضل

THE VIRTUOUS

Attending his father's lectures at the age of just three,
virtue was nurtured young until he was a virtuous sea
spilling from silent prostration to eloquent speech,
He was the remnants of the Prophets
like rivers and streams are to oceans and seas.

JAFAR

Like *Jafar* of old, this one swapped the sword
for the sciences with a mind as sharp as any.
Each teaching was a battle against ignorance
and each victory secured his legacy in the heavens.

NAMES OF AL-KADHIM

THE CALM

As calm as a breeze in a summer's night,
no chains can ruffle these feathers
nor darkness can make turbulent the tides
of his prostrating light.

THE DOOR TO FULFILLING ONE'S NEEDS

For every dungeon, every locked door faced,
he became a door open, a fulfilling fate
for every desperate heart that sits at his gate
beseeching God with this gifted name.

THE PURE SOUL

What do you call a caged dove that can still
bring peace to the hearts through iron bars?
What do you call a dove that can still fly
despite clipped wings?

MOSES

One *Moses* split the seas to unshackle
the Israelites from tyranny
but this one took on the chains himself
to unshackle the future for those
who believed.

NAMES OF AL-RIDHA

الرضا

THE ONE GOD IS CONTENT WITH

A whole empire, countless rivers and seas
the treasures of the world were laid at his feet
rolled out on Persian rugs
and yet his quarters remained rough
while he broke bread with the broken
and bequeathed knowledge like an ocean.

الصابر

THE PATIENT

Jesus walked for forty days, a battle with patience
al-Sabir abandoned Arabia for Persia,
until he was lifted in station.

غريب الغرباء
STRANGER AMONGST STRANGERS

His presence was enough to quell the game of thrones
but empires could only value him in gold coins
failing to appraise his true worth, declaring him heir but the
Almighty declared that first
The heirs of *Mohammed* are always apparent.

شاه خراسان
KING OF KHORASAN

As soon as the crescent of Muharram
saw its first morning he,
alongside *Khorasan* fell into mourning.
The most powerful army will always be the army of tears and
grief.

ALI

Have you wondered about the eighth *Ali* wonder?
Whether his fragrance would out-perfume
the hanging gardens of *Babylon*
or how high his dome would reach
if his devotees built it in the shape
of the great pyramid of *Giza*
or how the temple of *Artemis* was flattened by floods
but seas of lovers and angels still grace his courtyards
with enough doors for every heart to find him.

NAMES OF AL-JAWAD

محمد

MOHAMMED

The third *Mohammed*, the son of the golden chain
was born to be the ninth *Ali* to reign again,
like a shooting star of tender age
he lit up his father's eyes until they were seen to shine
like parallel moons blessing *Medina's* skylines.

التقي

THE PIOUS

The pious cannot be moved
for he has fortified his position like a river
between two mountains,
he continuously flows towards *Him* unobstructed
and the only way to stop a river
from quenching the thirst of the masses
is to poison it.

القانع
THE CONTENT

Twenty five years on earth was enough
for him to deem his glass half full.

الجواد
THE GENEROUS

How can you be the son of *Ali*
if your veins are not filled with
with the flow of generosity?

His heart was an open purse spilling
kindness wherever it could land,
be it to the passing bird
or the open palms of man.

NAMES OF AL-HADI

الهادي
THE GUIDE

At a tender age Caliphs would task teachers with
corrupting him
but instead they would end up becoming students of his.
"Where did he accumulate all this knowledge"
they would ask?
Where else? For the sons of the gate of knowledge
never left the city. They were born in it.

النقي
THE PURE

A diamond sparkles quietly on the inside
but reflects colourfully on the outside.
He was pure enough to bring colour
quietly to the world.

ALI

In twelve, you will find
four Mohammed's to three Ali's
for heaven must be seven
and he was three of three.

NAMES OF AL-ASKARI

حسن

HASSAN

Hassan would reappear from the lineage of *Hussain*
and the streets of *Samarra'* were to blessed with a
reincarnation
of *Medina's* Sibtayn.

العسكري

THE MILITANT

Bani *Hashem's* final generation was to be squeezed
between barracks and house arrest.
The predators were on a hunt,
anticipating a saviour to manifest
and that time will come when no military can contest
the son that *Al-Askari* would beget.

الصامت

THE QUIET

Like a bird building a nest in darkness, away from prying eyes,
he held the future of humanity between his palms
and the ripples of his quiet tongue.

NAMES OF AL-MAHDI

MOHAMMED

The one baptised by the *five* names
the jewel placed at the end time
The final *Mohammed*, like the first,
from the heart of *Mecca* will arise.

THE AWAITED

Here I weave each second by second into years
until oceans flow and winds come by
yet nothing is breathed between *you* and I.

الماء المعين
THE NATURAL SPRING OF WATER

When the air is thin at the edge of night
his presence serenades
the lungs that wait
for the promise that will come
when time falls sick and withers
of the oceans that his spring will deliver.

الغريم
THE COLLECTOR

The one who gathers the wounds of time
between two palms
and the heart that amasses the hurt of years
between its valves
a debt to the world that must be paid, in full.

الشريد

THE DISPLACED

The one who bleeds pain and prays
the one that compasses cannot find
the riddle solved only
when every soul realigns.

الخلف الصالح

THE RIGHTEOUS INHERITOR

I feel his presence growing between the thorns
giving life in a bloom
His presence bringing tides, a righteous coup
inside the stubborn heart that shifts in orbit
to allow enough sky for his justice, all of it.

الحجة
THE COMPLETION OF PROOF

His appearance shall be a trial
the jury will be the dead
and the living will be in denial
until pure hearts will beat his harbinger
and the sun itself will surrender its light to his smile.

بقية الله
THE REMNANT OF GOD

Every night as the moon peers down
and the sky adorns its twilight gown
I look between the hazy stars
and the shadows they disbar
for a glimpse of him, he who waits.

المهدي

THE RIGHTLY GUIDED ONE

What if the *Mahdi* appears inside us before he appears
outside
standing against the wall of our hearts,
the *kaaba* of understanding.
What if the second coming is the return
of the light that we were born with?

If my religion was poetry
His messenger would be the sun
and the book would be my lamp
for there is no day without night
and every star staring back
is a metaphor for things to come
and lessons from years gone by
If my religion was poetry
my sonnet would be a family
tree, green flags, the progeny
and every line would end with
Mohammed or Ali
alliterations and similes
If my religion was poetry
it would have no full stop
it would continue beyond the page
beyond the grave.

PRAISE FOR THE CHOSEN NAMES

"A breath-taking compilation of poems celebrating the lives of God's most beloved servants. Each sonnet of this book makes the heart yearn to be in the presence of the Prophet and his immaculate family!"
Shaykh Azhar Nasser, author and lecturer

"Such a beautiful and emotive piece of work! I love how Taher Adel delves deep into the root meaning and essential attributes of that name."
Nazmina Dhanji, author and founder of Arabiq Online

"The combination of profound linguistics and knowledge enlaced in succinct poetry, makes a beautiful and compelling read."
Saarah Bokhari, author and mentor

"It is difficult to quantify or portray this excellent book, *The Chosen Names* in a way that does it justice; part iconography, part mysticism, part lament, the author, Taher Adel, writes with a welcome freshness of heart, a clarity that resonates deep within, a manner that suggests hours of thought and prayer poured into each entry. This is a text that should find a place in every Muslim home, a daily reference, with the soaring beauty of each single name enough to give strength and courage for every day and for all those inevitable Karbalā moments of struggle that come as part of our daily course. These are, quite simply, some of the most beautiful reflections I have read on the precious names of the Ahl al-Bayt."
Father Christopher Clohessy, author and lecturer

"A triumph of literature.
You have never read about the Holy Household like this."
Nouri Sardar, author and poet

"I highly recommend you reading this book to appreciate the beauty and elegance of the blessed names of the Prophet and his household. The poetry in this book will take you through a journey of love and affection towards the noble Prophet and his progeny; and will teach you lessons of virtue, compassion and truth through *The Chosen Names*."
Dr Ali Al-Hilli, author and lecturer